Everyday People

Bettie Jordan Backus

Published by Beauty Shop Journals Publishing
P.O. Box 15
Moseley, Virginia 23120
www.shopbuyus.com

ISBN: 978-0-9719380-1-4

Library of Congress Cataloging-in-Publication Data
Names: Backus, Bettie Jordan, 2019-author.
Title: Everyday People/Bettie Jordan Backus
Description: Moseley, Virginia; Beauty Shop Journals Publishing, 2019.

First Printing: 2019

Ordering Information:

www.shopbuyus.com
amazon.com

Special discounts are available on quantity purchases by corporations, associations, educators, and others. For details, contact the publisher at the above listed address or through the website.

EVERYDAY PEOPLE

Bettie Jordan Backus

Erna Gilliam Robinson, Editor

Beauty Shop Journal Publishing
Richmond, Virginia

Dedication

This book is dedicated to my husband, who after God is the love of my life. It is dedicated to my twins, Chasten and Chaz, who have been my inspiration since the time of their premature birth in 1984. It is lovingly dedicated to my precious grandson, Joziah and my darling granddaughter, Jakayla. My parents, the late Rev. David A. Jordan and Ethel V. Jordan have always been my rock and inspiration. They taught me to find my place in this crazy world and not let anyone but God determine my destination or my worth.

I dedicate this and all of the *Beauty Shop Journal* publications to follow to my girls at the Beauty Shop. Special hats off to Janelle Jeffers and Liz Durity. These ladies have ensured that my coiffe is always stylish, bouncy and fabulous. Posthumously, I dedicate these pages to my dear friend and long-time stylist, Crystal Hudson, whose True Dreams Beauty Salon gave me my first adult Beauty Shop experience.

Finally, I dedicate this book to all of you who have encountered at least one of the persons that I spotlight in the pages that follow. It is my intent to inspire and enlighten each of you on the best way to survive *Everyday People*.

Contents

Bettie Jordan Backus

Preface

The older I get the more I realize that I keep meeting the same people repeatedly. Regardless of race, religion, background, gender or social status, people are inherently the same. I am not a therapist, nor do I have a degree in the fields of psychology, psychiatry or counseling. However, I have traveled extensively and during my career I have worked with some of the most brilliant minds. But inevitably I smile inside when I meet certain personality types. I have also managed quite a few people and have come to realize that more than anything, people share the same basic traits. They want to be accepted, acknowledged and respected. But most of all, they want to be appreciated. Once you learn this and follow *Bettie's Rules of People-ology*, your life and interaction with others will be much more rewarding.

What are *Bettie's Rules of People-ology?* They are quite simple. Treat people with respect. Acknowledge that differences in people make the world a better place. Be honest. Turn the other cheek...either end is fine. Pray for everyone regularly—both people you know and those that you don't—people you love and those that you don't. Wake up each morning with a thankful heart and an appreciation for the day ahead.

I completed research on a few personality types to determine if my approach is consistent with professionals. In some cases, I am consistent with the pros. In other instances, I approach people quite differently. My approach is strictly from my personal experiences and what works for me.

Here are a few of the personalities that I have observed and how I approach them. Some may work for you. Some may not. The one thing that I want you to take away from my experiences is that life is a journey. Many people that you meet along this journey will make a lasting impression or impact your life in some way. Remember that. If you apply *Bettie's Rules of People-ology* suggestions, you may just enjoy the journey a little more. And you will most certainly come to appreciate the differences that each of us possesses. But most of all remember that we are all just *EVERYDAY PEOPLE*.

ENJOY!

Bettie J. Barlow

Introduction

Everyday People is the first in *The Beauty Shop Journals* series. *The Beauty Shop Journals* idea was born out of the conversations that take place weekly during my visit to my favorite stylist, Janelle Jeffers. Like the infamous secret conversations among men in the barber shop, women discuss everything from politics, to world events, to new recipes, to investments, to parenting, or whatever spurs a good conversation. We inspire each other. We pray for each other. We listen to each other. But most of all, the time spent is informative, relaxing and extremely exhilarating. It's our time to release and enjoy the company of other ladies.

The inspiration for the series started as entries in my personal journal. However, through our weekly beauty shop conversations, I realized that others could benefit from my experiences and observations. We often share our pains, frustrations, losses and emotions. Some discussions continue for weeks.

Regardless of the topic, there is always one common theme, everyone wants to be heard, acknowledged and appreciated. Each woman brings her own unique perspective and experiences to each topic discussed. If the conversation is controversial, it may end with everyone giving a spirited *"high five"*. If emotional, hugs and even tears are commonplace. For confidential conversations, when there are only a couple of us, we usually commit to keeping each other in prayer.

Whatever the outcome, I always leave feeling upbeat and refreshed. My Pastor always references how God speaks to us in different places. How He always knows what's happening in our lives and can get a message to us, sometimes in the most unusual ways and by uncommon means. My experiences during my weekly visit to the beauty shop has been the source of inspiration not only for *Everyday People*, but for additional books to follow.

Although the inspiration for *The Beauty Shop Journals* in my weekly trek to the salon, it is my hope that the books will be enjoyed by all genders and age groups. In the book, each personality type is described. Then I give insights on how I have dealt with each. I also include a biblical reference for those of you who want to take your relationship a step farther.

To the young professional, learn from *"Motivated Mel"* and let your true colors shine through. You will be noticed. Although *"Mel"* is depicted as a male, each character is gender neutral. Adding a name brings the characters to life. There are just as many *"Gossipy Georges"* as *"Gossipy Gails"*.

If you are timid or shy and people tend to take advantage of your ideas because they know you won't speak up for yourself, be sure to read about *"Thieving Terry"* and some ways to counter those attempts to steal your thunder.

No one ever admits to being *"Dilly Diane"* or *"Dilly Dan"*. Who would? But we have all had those days, or at least those *"Ah ha"* moments.

If we are truly honest with ourselves, there are some of these traits in each of us. Why? Because at the end of the day, we are all just... *Everyday People*.

Know It All Ned

Meet *"Know It All Ned"*. Everyone has encountered at least one *Ned* in their lifetime. He's is an expert at everything. Regardless of the subject Ned has either done it, knows someone who has done it or is about to do it. Ned finishes your sentences. He diverts every conversation back to himself. When people see him coming, they take cover or swiftly move in a different direction.

How do I handle "Know It All Neds"?

o   First, I don't "handle" anyone. Ned usually lacks confidence in his own knowledge or abilities. Therefore, he seizes every opportunity to offer his unsolicited advice to others. He wants to hide his insecurities and self-doubt. One solution is to stroke his ego. Flatter him on his knowledge. Listen to Ned and thank him for his suggestion. But let him know that his approach may not be accepted by everyone. Where appropriate, caution him that "showing off" and making others feel small is not generally acceptable behavior.

o   Before making any type of presentation you can be sure that at least one *Ned* will be in the audience. Make sure you have researched the subject matter extremely well. That way, you'll be able to dispel any of *Ned's* outbursts or embarrassing comments.

o   If you are facilitating a meeting where *Ned* is in attendance, make sure to have an agenda. Listing each agenda item and the time allotted for each helps to keep the meeting on track and leaves little room for *Ned-isms*. If necessary, you can tell him that you appreciate his suggestions and will consider them for another discussion, if that's applicable. Again, the key is to be prepared.

o   If *Ned* continues to annoy, begin to ask him questions. "What's your source for that *Ned*?" Then ask if he is sure because your sources say otherwise. This will usually diffuse him.

o   Remember, everyone wants to feel appreciated. So, when confronted with a *"Know It All Ned"*, the best solution is not to insult him. However, if he continues to be a pain, shower him with facts. *Ned* will begin to realize that he does not *"know it all"*.

A Biblical Reference to Consider:

> *A joyful heart is good medicine, but a crushed spirit dries up the bones.*
> Proverbs 17:22

Willie One Way

Next, there's *"Willie One Way"*. Willie has been employed by the same company for years. He's extremely dedicated. He learned most of his tasks from his predecessor and has continued the same practice for many years. Technology has changed. Bosses have come and gone. But *Willie* continues to use that old ten-key adding machine. Even though you have introduced him to Microsoft Excel and Access he continues to plug away on the memorized key pad. You have created templates and continue to send him to classes each year to learn the latest and greatest features and upgrades. But Willie continues with his old methods. He uses that 10-key to double check the Excel spreadsheet formulas.

What's the best way to cope with *"Willie One Way"?*

o   Ask Willie why he performs his task that way. His response will be: "We've always done it this way". But here's the kicker. More than likely Willie doesn't know why he performs a task a certain way.

> I am reminded of the old story of the husband who would always take on the task of baking the Thanksgiving ham. Each year, regardless of the size of the ham, he would cut off about an inch of each end of the ham before placing it in the baking pan and placing it in the oven to bake. One Thanksgiving while observing his father carry out the chop/chop tradition, his son asked: "Hey Dad, why do you always cut off both ends of the ham?" The father responded, "It's a family tradition that I learned from Grandma. She always did it this way".

> Being an inquisitive young chap, the son called his grandmother and asked: "Grammy, why do you chop off both ends of the ham before placing it in the oven". The grandmother replied, "Darling, I used to do that years ago. You see, back when your grandfather and I were first married our oven was very small. Your grandfather would always buy a ham that was much too large to fit into the small oven. So, I would cut it off at both ends and use those ends as seasoning for the vegetables. One end was used for the pot of greens. I put the other end in the pot of beans."

> Often, when we don't know *"why"* something is done. But if we never question it, we continue traditions that are no longer relevant.

- Involve Willie, as much as reasonably possible, in your change process. Resistance to change is often due to the lack of understanding of the reason for the change.

- Always acknowledge and or reward Willie when he makes small steps that will lead to him using new processes. In my example, when Willie began to use Excel, I made sure to give him a pat on the back for trying something new. I also applauded the fact that his work was always accurate. Although I knew that he was still using the adding machine to check behind the formulas in the spreadsheet, I praised his progress.

- Help Willie visualize what the change will look like. If you are in a non-competitive market (e.g. a government agency, school, university, etc.), have him visit a sister city, a school in a different jurisdiction or a college or university where the new method that you are introducing has already been successful. Schedule a meeting with his counterpart at that organization and allow him to spend as much time as possible. For corporations, see if you can find training or another organization in the same industry with a proven track record for the new method. Find articles or YouTube videos to share.

- Willie is not necessarily resisting change. He may be resisting the loss of his job. I have worked in technology for over thirty years. What I have found is people have a fear that once new technology is introduced, they will lose their jobs. What I try to relay is that technology will only enhance what they do. In most cases, they will not be replaced (at least not due to the introduction of new technology). Often, because more and better information is available, they end up having more work and responsibility because of the new doors that open. New opportunities often follow. Emphasize that the change has growth potential because the company is moving forward. And as the company grows, Willie will have the opportunity to grow as well.

Once again, everyone wants to feel appreciated. Work with Willie. He's usually a dedicated employee who wants to be appreciated for both his commitment to the organization and his spirt of excellence. *Willie One Way* can easily become *Practically Perfect Paul* if given the opportunity. Help Willie soar!

A Biblical Reference to Consider:

> *But if anyone has the world's goods and sees his brother in need, yet closes his heart against him, how does God's love abide in him?*
>
> 1 John 3:17

Kiss Up Kathy

Ever met a *"Kiss Up Kathy"*? *Kiss Up* says "yes" to everything the boss asks and instructs. Even when she has a solution that can cut costs and save time, *Kiss Up* goes along with the plan. Often working as a double agent among team members, the boss will engage *Kiss Up* to eavesdrop on co-workers and bring back information. While she appears to be *"Jolly JoAnn"* to her colleagues, *"Kiss Up"* will spill every detail of her co-workers' discussion in order to win praise from senior management. *"Kiss Up"* is always the first to arrive to work in the morning and usually one of the last to leave.

Once you have identified *"Kiss Up Kathy"*, you should:

- Never divulge any of your personal information or anything that you don't want repeated to other friends, in the office and definitely not to senior management.

- Remain cool when you detect that she is trying to obtain information from you. Do not lose your temper.

- If you manage a *"Kiss Up Kathy"*, make sure she has enough work to keep her busy. This will eliminate or at least reduce her "chat time". If her behavior persists, explain why such behavior is unacceptable and counterproductive. Where appropriate, ensure that her performance evaluation outlines proper conduct and work ethic.

- Always keep a paper trail and follow up work-related conversations with an email. Even if *"Kiss Up"* does not respond to the email, you will have documentation as proof of your discussions.

- Keep all conversations professional when dealing with *"Kiss Up Kathy"*.

You can dispel *"Kiss Up Kathy's"* activities by not engaging in her unprofessional behavior.

A Biblical Reference to Consider:

> *And no wonder, for even Satan disguises himself as an angel of light.*
> 2 Corinthians 11:14

Gossipy Gail

There's an adage: *"the same dog that carries the bone, buries the bone"*. In other words, you need to be careful with whom you share your secrets and innermost thoughts. *"Gossipy Gail"* will tell all to anyone who listens. Gail is always in the break room catching all the juicy office gossip. She then selectively spreads information, often adding a little extra spice here and there to make the tale more interesting.

Gossipy preys on juicy tidbits about personal friends and senior management and loves being "in the know" and the storehouse for all news. Although Gail spreads the information on everyone else, usually her colleagues know very little about her personal life.

When confronted by "Gossipy", try the following:

o If you learn that the gossip is about you, remain calm. Take a few moments, step away and compose yourself. If a situation has occurred that you feel will result in office gossip, get ahead of the story and make sure your version is conveyed, if you so desire. Dispel any malicious or uncomplimentary chatter before it spreads throughout the organization. Remain professional. If the rumor is extremely vicious, shut it down as soon as possible. Work to find out who started the rumor and speak with them privately.

o Speak directly to *Gossipy* and have a one-on-one conversation. Tell *Gossipy* that you would appreciate her not spreading false information about you. If the gossip is true, let her know that you would never disclose personal information about her, and you would appreciate the same courtesy.

o If you have told *Gossipy* information in confidence and she decided to spread it, let her know that you do not appreciate her breaking your confidence.

o Moving forward let that be a lesson. Even if your co-worker or friend is not a gossip be careful when sharing personal information. Even your closest friend may have someone else with whom they confide. It only takes one person to tell one person and your secret will spread exponentially.

o Be a role model for others by not engaging in gossip. Ignore *Gail* when she begins to chinwag.

A Biblical Reference to Consider:

There are six things that the LORD hates, seven that are an abomination to him: haughty eyes, a lying tongue, and hands that shed innocent blood, a heart that devises wicked plans, feet that make haste to run to evil, a false witness who breathes out lies, and one who sows discord among brothers.

Proverbs 6:16-19

Tardy Tammy

"Tardy Tammy" is always late. She *never* arrives to work on time. She's always late for meetings and is disruptive when she enters the room. Although *Tardy* is late every morning, she wastes an additional half hour getting settled in. In the winter she removes her coat, hat, scarf and gloves. Then she sashays over to the break room to grab a cup of coffee and heat the *Chick fil a* biscuit that she picked up on the way in. Next, she stops by *Gossipy Gail's* desk to see if anything interesting happened before she arrived. She finally settles into her desk and works for about an hour before taking her morning break. Her fifteen-minute break, which lasts a half hour, ends very close to lunch time.

Therefore, about forty-five minutes later she's back in the breakroom heating her lunch. Some days she brings the lunch back to her desk and gobbles it down while reading the morning paper or surfing the Internet. However, if *Gossipy Gail* has some interesting story, she'll remain in the break room and the two will chat while munching on last night's leftovers.

After about forty-five minutes of conversation and food, *Tardy Tammy* leaves the building on her "lunch break" to run those errands that "must be completed" today.

If you have *Tardy Tammy* as an employee, try the following:

o Discuss Tammy's tardiness with her. Let her know that you noticed that she is consistently late. Listen to her reason. Perhaps she is a single mom and must wait for the school bus before she can leave for work. If this is the case, discuss a flexible work schedule which will allow her to arrive a little later in the mornings and stay later in the evenings.

o If this is not the case and Tammy is just a late person, identify the behavior and develop an action plan. Review the plan periodically (usually once a month initially to see if she is adhering to the plan).

o If Tammy begins to show improvement, reward the improved behavior. If she does not improve, tie her tardiness to her performance evaluation and detail the consequences of continued abuse.

o Always respect your employee's privacy. But likewise, ensure that they respect their job and your authority to act if the unsatisfactory behavior continues.

A Biblical Reference to Consider:

"You also must be ready, for the Son of Man is coming at an hour you do not expect."
Luke 12:40

Practically Perfect Paul

"Practically Perfect Paul" is the ideal employee. Although no one is perfect, Paul is as close to a perfect employee as you will find anywhere. He arrives to work at least a half hour early. Paul grabbed his *Starbucks* on the ride to work and flips on his laptop to allow it to boot up while he removes his coat and gloves. By the time the laptop boots up, he has removed the report that he sent to the printer in his office last night for a final edit and review before turning it in to the boss upon his/her arrival.

Paul then begins to research the new concept that he heard about on the news while dressing this morning. He wants to see if the company can take advantage of the concept and if it would be cost effective. Once he has completed enough research, he compiles the information; adds a few graphs and charts for emphasis and completes his assessment in time for the morning meeting.

What do you do with a *"Practically Perfect Paul"*?

o   Reward him for his dedication to the job.

o   Use him as a mentor or role model for younger, less experienced employees on the job or youth in your personal life.

o   Make sure to incorporate his ideas into the overall strategy of your division and/or the organization, where applicable.

o   If bonuses are awarded, ensure that he is at the top of the list.

o   Work with Paul to develop his career plan and training options. You need to retain "practically perfect" employees. Keep and allow "practically perfect" friends to be your personal role model.

A Biblical Reference to Consider:

> *You therefore must be perfect, as your heavenly Father is perfect.*
> Matthew 5:48

Dilly Diane

"Dilly Diane" is one of the nicest people you'll ever meet. However, after just one conversation you realize that her elevator does not go to the top floor. She's so dilly that sometimes you avoid having a conversation with her because it's just too much effort. Everyone wonders why Dilly still has a job. But then, she probably has qualities that are not apparent to the mortal eye. Often Dilly is the daughter of a friend or the senior partner's ex-wife. Dilly may be extremely gorgeous and gains the proverbial "gentlemen's pat on the back" from the boss's colleagues and golf buddies.

What should you do when you manage a Diane or have one for a "bestie"?

○ If Diane is your employee, always remember there has only been one Einstein. Make sure she is trained for the tasks and responsibilities that you assign to her. Diane is a dedicated employee. And even though she may be four short of a six pack, she's loyal. Reward her loyalty.

○ If your Diane does not speak up and ask questions when you "know" she doesn't understand the assignment, make sure you ask her (in private, after the meeting), if she understands. If she says "Yes" but has the "deer caught in the headlight" look in her eyes, have her repeat her understanding back to you. Then explain it again. Tell her to write it down, if necessary.

○ If your Diane is the type who asks "obvious" questions in meetings and everyone else is annoyed by her lack of understanding, ask if anyone else has a question. If not, dismiss the group and assist her privately to curtail any embarrassment. If Diane continually does not understand the assignments or is unable to keep up, maybe a different job within the department, one with less responsibility, is the solution. If not, you may need to have Diane seek other employment options within the organization.

○ If *Dilly* is your girlfriend. Remember, you are judged by the company that you keep. Do not embarrass her in public. Make subtle suggestions on behaviors or choices that don't hurt her feelings. *Dianes* are usually nice people. They are just a bit naïve. Do not use her. She's usually the one who picks up the tab on "girl's night out". Do not take advantage of her giving spirit. And if you see others taking advantage of Diane, alert her. If you know the perpetrator, speak to them on Diane's behalf. That is what a "real" friend would do.

A Biblical Reference to Consider:

> *And what you have heard from me in the presence of many witnesses entrust to faithful men who will be able to teach others also.*
>
> 2 Timothy 2:2

"No-Nonsense Nannette" comes off as being somewhat of a prude. She's usually a loner. She's quiet, yet extremely focused on whatever task is assigned to her. Nannette is brilliant. She's usually quite attractive and always surprises everyone at formal company events. While at work she dresses extremely well. Brooks Brothers suits, heels that are not too tall, yet obviously expensive, hair always perfectly coiffed. But at those afterhours events, all bets are off and Nannette is the bell of the ball.

Her work is always meticulous. Her comments are always appropriate and politically correct. She's abreast of the latest news and is always on point when called upon in meetings or for a last-minute project.

Working with Nannette should be a joy. Having her as a friend can prove to be rewarding. Here are some tips:

o Draw upon Nannette's knowledge and experience. Because she is attractive and well put together, people will usually respond favorably to her. Have her make the presentations to senior management.

o As with *Practically Perfect*, allow Nannette to mentor some of the younger and/or less experienced employees. Introduce her to your teenage daughter (or son in the case of a *No-Nonsense Nathan*). It's interesting how teens tend to listen to stylish, polished adults.

o Reward her if she is an employee.

o She would enjoy being a part of your organization. Invite her to join your book club or to join your golf buddies (Nannette or Nathan). They usually don't engage because no one asks or invites them. People tend to shy away from *Nannettes* and Nathans because they don't appear to be approachable. Approach! Approach!

o Appreciate her or him.

o Promote them.

o Allow them to grow.

A Biblical Reference to Consider:

The plans of the diligent lead surely to abundance, but everyone who is hasty comes only to poverty.

Proverbs 21:5

Mommy Meagan

"Mommy Meagan" is the working mother who does it all. She's been through a divorce and the child support and alimony payments don't leave enough extra cash at the end of the month. She normally gets everything done on time and still has time to collect for the school's parent/teacher association fundraiser or sell Girl Scout cookies.

She stays focused because the job is her survival kit. Meagan is likeable and always has new pictures of the kids to share. She tends to avoid *Gossipy Gail*. Although from time to time she finds some of the juicy tidbits extremely intriguing.

Here are a few tips for the Mommy *Meagans* in your life:

o If Meagan is your friend, and if you are either single with no kids or an empty nester, be patient with her. Compliment her on her appearance and mothering skills. On those days when she appears to be overwhelmed, assist her by offering to watch the kids for a few hours to allow her some down time. On her birthday or other special occasions where the two of you exchange gifts, purchase a spa gift card and offer to watch the kids when she decides to redeem it. If it takes too long for her to redeem the card, suggest that she uses it when you notice that she needs a break. If you are also a mother, schedule play dates for the kids from time to time. You can help each other. If there is a significant difference in your children's ages, give your child a special treat, extra privileges or even cash, if possible, for assisting with babysitting.

o If Meagan is a co-worker, be patient and compliment the millions of baby pictures. Also, if you can afford it, purchase some of the Girl Scout cookies and fundraiser odds and ends.

o If Meagan is your employee, be as lenient as you can with her. Do not over compensate because you'll risk showing favoritism and not being fair to the employees who are not mothers or do not have Meagan's level of responsibility. If necessary, allow her to use flex time to attend recitals, school meetings, child care issues, sick days, etc. Since most Meagans are loyal workers, reward her where feasible.

A Biblical Reference to Consider:
> *Whatever you do, work heartily, as for the Lord and not for men, knowing that from the Lord you will receive the inheritance as your reward. You are serving the Lord Christ.*
> Colossians 3:23-24

"Motivated Mel" is the typical millennial. He's aggressive. He is not afraid to share his opinions and ideas. He's not afraid to challenge his superiors. He wants his work to have "meaning". He's not in it just to earn a salary. He wants to make an impact. An impact on what? On whatever is in his heart. The community. The world. He doesn't look at organizational structure. He wants a mentor. He wants to belong. He wants his co-workers to feel like his extended family.

Mel is extremely tech savvy. He doesn't understand how *"One Way Willie"* can be so far behind in his knowledge of technology. However, he is always eager to assist Willie. Although initially leery of Mel's intentions, Willie appreciates his assistance and doesn't feel intimidated when he reaches out to help.

Mel lives for social media. Since he is "truly" a millennial and doesn't believe in doing things just because they have always been done a certain way, he and Willie often clash on non-technical issues. But at the end of the day, they are back to being pals. Because Mel believes his job should be measured by "work completed" and "quality of work", he would prefer teleworking. The "in the office from 9 to 5" is not his preference and he has completed a study that shows how productivity can be improved with a hybrid work schedule. Mel wants to take as many classes as possible. He wants to continually learn and grow. He works hard and craves recognition. Although he loves his job, he only plans to stay for about three years before moving on to his next opportunity.

What do you do for a Motivated Mel?

o Keep him motivated by ensuring that he receives bonuses and/or rewards for his performance.

o Ensure that a career path is developed for Mel and the other employees under your management and use him as a mentor or example whenever applicable. Be careful not to go overboard with the compliments, however. Too much attention to one employee can cause issues with others who are motivated, but not quite as obvious as Mel.

o Use Mel's ideas whenever possible and make sure that he knows that he is valued by the company.

o You will notice that his enthusiasm will begin to rub off on other employees when they see the fruits of his labor.

A Biblical Reference to Consider:

The glory of young men is their strength, but the splendor of old men is their gray hair.
Proverbs 20:29

Ready Ricky

What is *"Ready Ricky"*, ready for? "Ready Ricky" is ready to retire. Ricky is in his mid-sixties. He and his wife have been married since college and are now empty nesters. Ricky is the typical boomer. He has worked his entire life. He rarely takes vacation. He has been loyal to the company. He's been dependable. He has a strong work ethic. He follows the rules. However, he will voice his opinion when his personal values or even the laws have been compromised. He's a straight shooter. He sets goals and has attained most of them. He contributed regularly to his 401K. Therefore, he and his wife are financially stable and will be able to begin chipping away at that bucket list that they created after attending the movie with Morgan Freeman and Jack Nicholson. He doesn't ask for much.

He knows how to make the best out of each situation and mentors many of those hired after him. He's mentally focused. He's an honorable church-going man. He's often more of a liberal thinker than people realize. However, he knows how to keep those thoughts to himself in mixed company. He's a team player and extremely disciplined in his daily activities. He's a family man. Although family always comes first, the job never suffers. His priorities are in order.

What do you do for *"Ready Ricky"*?

o   This one can be a bit tricky. Most of the time *Ready Ricky's* want to retire. Knowing this fact, some managers tend to include *Ricky* in early retirement plans when trying to downsize. This approach could backfire. Some Ricky's want to retire. But they want to do it in their own time. Others will be fine with the early out. Work to "know your employees" to make sure you understand which is correct for your *Ready Ricky*. If pushed to retire, *Ready Ricky* may become *Resentful Ricky* and fill betrayed for all his years of loyalty. This may be the one time that he does not make his feelings apparent. However, because he has been with the company for many years, he may work behind the scenes to cause issues that won't be apparent until he's gone. For example, there may be one process that he is the only person aware of its importance to the overall operations. He performs that process every day. He's been doing it for so long that it's just a normal part of his daily routine. It has never been documented and because of turnover and management changes over the years, no one was aware of the task. However, when Ricky leaves, that process will no longer be executed. Therefore, unforeseen issues arise that no one knows how to resolve because the cause is not apparent.

o Show Ricky that you appreciate him. When he finally goes to Human Resources to initiate his exit plan, make sure to plan an elaborate retirement celebration. Pull out all the bells and whistles. He'll appreciate the gesture and will more than likely mention that "thing" that he was doing to ensure continuity of operations.

o Listen to Ricky's suggestions. Because he has been with the company for years, he will most likely have more institutional knowledge than most of the people on staff. Therefore, his input can be invaluable.

o However, if you are new to the organization and *Ready Ricky* reports to you, be careful not to feel intimidated by his knowledge. Especially if you are younger, *Ready Ricky's* have the tendency to take charge. Make sure you establish your boundaries upon arrival. Otherwise, *Ready* can become a royal pain. Use his knowledge to your advantage, not his.

o Help Ricky retire with dignity…

A Biblical Reference to Consider:

> *So we do not lose heart. Though our outer self is wasting away, our inner self is being re-newed day by day.*
>
> 2 Corinthians 4:16

Jolly JoAnne

Jolly JoAnne is Generation X personified. She appreciates fun in the workplace. She has a pleasing personality and is a joy to be around. She arrives on time and usually completes her assignments on schedule and within budget. She works hard and plays hard. She's the one who everyone looks forward to arriving at the office party to get the festivities started. She is independent, resourceful and extremely self-contained. She adapts well to change and can usually influence others to get on the band wagon. She's open to all types of people.

Regardless of race, gender preference, religion or belief, Jolly is in your corner. JoAnn is comfortable with the latest gadgets. She doesn't run out and buy every widget on the market. But she can usually figure out how to make things work. JoAnn always succeeds. She moves up the corporate ladder with ease. Most of her colleagues are happy for her because they know she has earned her way.

Age is usually the only difference between *Jolly JoAnne* and *Candice the Cheerleader*. *Jolly JoAnne* is usually younger and less experienced than Candice. Jolly has only been out of college for a short period of time and this may be her first full time job.

How do you work with Jolly JoAnne?

o You do just that. You work with her. You teach her the ropes and help her grow. Since *JoAnn* is competent and comfortable with the latest gadgets, have her develop training for others in the department. Ensure that she is not intimidating to other staff members by scheduling a series of training sessions within the department. Let some of the more seasoned staffers train on an established process or procedure. Then give Jolly the reigns and let her show off her techy skills. Everyone wins.

o As a co-worker, embrace her cheerful personality and allow it to blossom within the organization and be a blessing to others.

o If JoAnn is your friend, embrace her enthusiasm. Ask her to assist you with parties and projects where her talents will take the event to the next level. She usually has unique ideas that add just enough flare to make the occasion extra special.

A Biblical Reference to Consider:
Then he said to them, "Go your way. Eat the fat and drink sweet wine and send portions to anyone who has nothing ready, for this day is holy to our Lord. And do not be grieved, for the joy of the LORD is your strength." Nehemiah 8:10

Narcissistic Nadine

Then there's *"Narcissistic Nadine"*. No matter the situation, Nadine will find a reason to complain, whine or nag. The temperature is too cold in the winter and too hot in the summer. The boss is always overlooking her and giving everyone else the promotion. Nadine is selfish. Regardless of what's happening within your friendship, the corporation, organization or situation, Nadine will always find a reason to complain and then find a way to make the outcome benefit her.

She is toxic in the work environment because if not controlled, she can be the rotten apple that spoils the entire batch. She never lets up.

What do you do when you have a Narcissistic Nadine in your life?

o If Nadine is your girlfriend, when you see the nagging behavior starting to take over, take cover. Run Forrest, run. Running serves a two-fold purpose. Number one, you are out of the way of the negativity. Number two, Nadine can be negative all by herself.

o If Nadine is your employee, compliment her on her work, if appropriate. Ask what issues she's having with the job. Note those and work with her to develop an action plan. If she continues to nag and complain, refer to the plan and discuss ways of revising it. If neither works, move to the next step within your Human Resources policy manual. Remember, Nadine's negative behavior will tend to rub off on the other employees. Avoid that at all costs.

o If your wife is the nagger, shower her with compliments and gifts. That will usually stop the nagging, for at least a while. If that doesn't work, join her girlfriends and run, Forest, run. Find a quiet place in the house. Create your man cave (or woman cave if you have a Narcissistic Norris) and use it as your escape room. If all else fails, go to the local bar and have a cold one. The only problem with that solution, however, is that when you return home, she'll have something else to nag about (i.e. the fact that you went out drinking).

Hubby, wife or employer you can always work to keep Nadine busy. Keeping her busy will reduce the nagging. She won't have the time or energy.

A Biblical Reference to Consider:

Pride goes before destruction, and a haughty spirit before a fall.

Proverbs 16:18

John the Judge

"John the Judge" finds fault in everyone except himself. John has unrealistic expectations of others. Regardless of how well a co-worker completed an assignment, it's never good enough. John judges everything from his co-workers' clothing, to his friend's choice in vehicles to the type of home in which they live. Never mind work, he's too busy finding fault in all other aspects of their lives. Having John as a boss is extremely frustrating. Regardless of the quality of the project, it's never good enough for *"Judging John"*.

How do you handle John?

o   If John is judging you, it usually has to do with him coming in touch with his own shortcomings and dysfunction. Try not to take it personally. His judgment has nothing to do with you and everything to do with him. There is a strong possibility that you have something that he wants. He sees you with it and determines that if he had it, he would treat it differently. Again, it's John's issue not yours.

o   John may be depressed and is projecting his negative feelings on to the people around him. Try having compassion and treating him with love and respect. You may see a change in his attitude.

o   Show John gratitude for assisting you with "seeing the light" in a situation or circumstance. Make John feel valuable.

o   Look for the "good" in John. He may be going through a season where he doesn't feel good about himself. Therefore, he releases that negativity into the atmosphere. Find one of his good qualities and expound upon it.

o   *Tao Te Ching,* a Chinese classic text which was written by Laozi in 6th century BC, states: *"What is a good man, but a bad man's teacher? What is a bad man but a good man's job?"* Learn from John. Learn how not to be judgmental. And learn how people will see and acknowledge you if you become John.

o   Do not allow John's judgmental ways to become a part of who you are. When we spend too much time with negative and judgmental people, we begin to act and think like them. If you find yourself becoming John, stop and reflect on the good things in your life.

A Biblical Reference to Consider:

"Judge not, that you be not judged. For with the judgment you pronounce you will be judged, and with the measure you use it will be measured to you."

Matthew 7:1-2

Bob the Bully

From childhood to adulthood there's always a bully in the crowd. *Bob the Bully* shows up on every job. As a child he's usually the big kid. Therefore, he can intimidate all who are smaller in stature. As an adult, Bob is the person on the job who pretends to be "in the know". However, he usually has very low self-esteem and uses his size or position to push people around.

How do you deal with a bully? Many books have been written, studies completed, and documentaries created to discuss the best way to handle a bully.

Here are a few of my thoughts and beliefs:

For Adults:

o Avoid bullies whenever possible. I am not suggesting that you run away. But as you may have learned in traffic school, all accidents can be avoided. Likewise, once you have determined that an individual is a bully, avoid them as much as humanly possible. Don't make it obvious that you are avoiding them. That may result in additional bullying.

o Remain calm and try to ignore their unsuitable and unwelcomed behavior. This is probably the hardest of all because bullies get a rush from causing a scene and publicly embarrassing you. They usually do it because "they can". Bullies will target you if they know they will get a reaction. Work hard "not" to give them what they are looking for from you.

o If you use social media, simply block their profile and remove any connections to the person. Once you remove them, be leery of new friend requests. The bully may create a new profile as a means of staying in contact with you.

o Ignore them. Again, bullies target people who they know they can intimidate. They may resort to name calling or embarrassing you in public. If they see that you are getting upset, they will escalate. Think about how silly they look if you just walk away. They are left acting out and looking foolish. You will be the adult and more sensible person by not showing your emotions.

o Do not feel compelled to explain yourself to a bully. The more you talk to them, the more you fuel their ego and open yourself up to additional harassment, embarrassment and ridicule.

o Try using humor in a situation where they have embarrassed you. If they are trying to embarrass you by making a joke at your expense, laugh along with them. Say, "Thanks, Bob" as nicely as you can. Then turn and walk away. That will take the sting out of the taunt. That will show the bully that you don't care.

o At work, if the situation escalates to a point where you can no longer avoid or handle the behavior, speak with your manager. If the manager is the problem or if they do not assist you, consult your Human Resources department for assistance.

For Children and Young Adults:

I will not make recommendations because each situation is different. I would suggest that you speak with your children openly and regularly. If you have a child with special needs or who may not fit into what kids consider "normal", do not hesitate to discuss bullying with them. Bullies and bullying can be extremely dangerous, and you should be aware of any such behavior when it comes to your child.

A Biblical Reference to Consider:

> *Be strong and courageous. Do not fear or be in dread of them, for it is the LORD your God who goes with you. He will not leave you or forsake you.*
>
> Deuteronomy 31:6

Stand your ground!

Do Nothing Dave

Do Nothing Dave" does just what his name implies. He does nothing. All day, *Dave* puts on the appearance of doing his job when he actually spends most of his time surfing the Internet. He arrives on time. He clocks out at 5:00 sharp and is the first to the parking lot. He volunteers for every conceivable activity to avoid "real work". How does he get away with it? He's a nice guy. He's neat. Because he is always on time, he gives the appearance of being the perfect employee. He always runs errands for the boss.

His job does not require a tremendous amount of effort. Therefore, he knows when to jump in just in time to get it done. He appears to be efficient. Regardless of what the boss needs, he's *"Johnny on the spot"* to run to Office Max for that toner cartridge so the boss can finish the important report. He'll make a deli run when the meeting runs over, and the boss orders take out. He knows how to fix the printer in *Dilly Diane's* office. He knows enough about office politics to stay just inside of the boundaries.

What do you do with Dave?

- o If Dave is a co-worker, before you do anything make sure your work is complete and that you have no outstanding projects or tasks. If you are working with Dave on a project and he is not pulling his weight, let Dave know that you need his assistance to keep the project on schedule. If Dave continues to slack off, make sure you document your discussion. The next step will be to contact your manager. Make sure that he or she is made aware that Dave is not pulling his weight and as a result, the project completion date is in jeopardy.

- o If Dave is the type who is trying to get you to pull his weight, immediately say "No". If you do it once, Dave will become dependent on you completing his tasks and you'll become his crutch.

- o If Dave is your employee, don't fall for the morning coffee and donut trick to compensate for his work. Set your boundaries. Ensure that his assignments are outlined and clear. Make sure that his performance evaluations reflect expectations and then hold him accountable. Ensure that you are developing and expounding upon Dave's strengths. The problem could be that he is not being challenged and has become bored with his current position. Spice up the assignment and give him an incentive to be motivated. Document the behavior. Communicate your observances with Dave. Set a timeline for behavior improvement. Have scheduled follow up meetings. If this approach does not work, it may be time for Dave to take his donuts and coffee and find employment elsewhere.

A Biblical Reference to Consider:

> *For even when we were with you, we would give you this command: If anyone is not willing to work, let him not eat.*
>
> 2 Thessalonians 3:10

Aggressive Angela

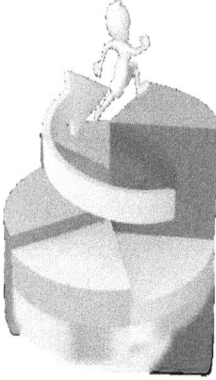

"Aggressive Angela" is working her way up the corporate ladder and doesn't care who she steps on or over to get there. She will do anything for a promotion. She'll sabotage anyone to move ahead. Angela is a loner by choice. She has no close girlfriends because she competes with everyone in both her personal and professional life. Therefore, no one trusts her. She will eventually make it to the top. However, once she gets there, she'll realize how lonely she is because of the people she squashed on her way up the corporate ladder. Angela will eventually become the Sr. VP, CEO, CFO or Chief Widget Maker. By age fifty she'll realize that she has made many sacrifices and is still unfulfilled.

What do you do with *"Aggressive Angela"*?

o Make sure she has assignments that are challenging and that will help your organization grow and move forward. Angela is eager to grow. She will make the most out of each opportunity. Be careful with Angela. Like *Toxic Tommy*, Angela will compete to stay on top. If you are a co-worker, she will steal your ideas and incorporate them into her own. Unlike *Thieving Terry*, she's crafty enough to camouflage your ideas so that it would be hard to prove where they originated.

o Angela trusts no one and no one trusts her. She has very few friends. She is always competing with everyone, including herself, to get to the top. No one is exempt from being trampled. She'll bypass her manager and go directly to his/her colleagues and superior to get what she wants. Organizational chain of command means nothing to her.

o Angela usually realizes how lonely she is on holidays or when she reaches the age where childbirth is too risky. When everyone else is planning family dinners and holiday celebrations, she's in her office working on the project that will take her to the next level. One day she wakes up and realizes that her girlfriends are anticipating grandchildren and she has never married. She has amassed a huge bank account, lives a lush life and has the best that life has to offer. However, she is usually quite lonely.

o There is really nothing that you can do for Angela except be there for her when she needs a friend. However, be cautious. You may have something that she wants. Hold on to your spouse or mate. Aggression is aggression.

A Biblical Reference to Consider:

> *"All things are lawful for me," but not all things are helpful. "All things are lawful for me," but I will not be enslaved by anything.*
>
> 1 Corinthians 6:12

"Opinionated Oliver" just can't keep his thoughts to himself. Regardless of the subject he has an opinion. Right, wrong or indifferent, Oliver is going to be heard. He imposes on everyone's conversation. He's the guy who shoots down everyone else's proposal or suggestion. Oliver has rubbed so many people the wrong way that even if he has a valuable opinion, most will never know because everyone has learned to tune him out. He's annoying because he believes he is "always" right. If you say the sky is blue, he'll respond that it's indigo.

Here's how to deal with Oliver:

- Acknowledge Oliver's opinion. But do not allow his opinion to change yours unless there is a valid reason to do so.

- Take Oliver with a grain of salt. If you agree, fine. If not. No problem. You are an intelligent being. Just as Oliver has opinion, you have your own. Listen, then move on.

- Do not take what Oliver says to heart. It's just his opinion. Everybody has one. When Oliver chimes in with his opinion, be confident enough to tell him that although you see his point of view, you would approach the situation in a different manner.

- Opinionated Oliver usually doesn't have many friends because people grow tired of his narrow views.

A Biblical Reference to Consider:

> *For everyone who exalts himself will be humbled, and he who humbles himself will be exalted."*
>
> Luke 14:11

Thieving Terry

"Thieving Terry" is the person who steals your ideas and attempts to make them his own. Or he's the cousin who finds out what your kids want for Christmas and purchases the items for his kids, especially if he knows that you can't afford to buy them. He's the same person who will lie when asked— "who took the last slice of apple pie" even though he heard you ask to save that last piece while you took out the trash.

Terry wants what everyone else has. He's usually the one who can afford to purchase even the most expensive items. But he's usually not creative enough to think of the best gifts on his own. Therefore, he steals ideas from everyone else.

How do you deal with Thieving Terry?

o   At work, always document and date your ideas and projects. Outline the details so that it will be impossible to deny that the original idea was yours.

o   Avoid sharing your ideas before submitting them for approval.

o   If you haven't followed the first two points and your idea is stolen by Terry, confront Terry in private. Stay calm. If you are uncomfortable with confronting him in person or feel that you will be unable to keep your composure, send him an email. If appropriate, cc: your manager.

o   If you are in a meeting with Terry, ask questions about the idea. Continue to dig. Then add in your concepts. It will become obvious that you are on top of the idea and should take the lead on the project.

o   Talk to your boss before you work on a new proposal or idea. Let him or her know that you want to develop a new concept. Set expectations (e.g. how you will build the prototype, a draft schedule of events/timeline, outline of the overall approach). Therefore, if Terry tries to steal your idea or take credit, your boss will know.

o   In your personal life, be careful about the information that you share with Terry. A real friend wouldn't steal from you.

A Biblical Reference to Consider:

> *Let the thief no longer steal, but rather let him labor, doing honest work with his own hands, so that he may have something to share with anyone in need.*
>
> Ephesians 4:28

Jealous Joan

"Jealous Joan" tries to keep up with the Joneses. She often doesn't realize or care that she and the Joneses may be in totally different tax brackets. She goes to everyone's open house, trying to find ideas that she can use in her home. She's also the one who always asks where you bought that dress or who does your hair. Where did you get your shoes? How much did they cost? She is never satisfied with herself or her own possessions.

Everything that everyone else has always looks better. Therefore, she "must" have it. Trying to keep up with others has often placed Joan in debt. But she doesn't care. She scrapes and saves to make sure that she gets whatever everyone else has.

Irish author, Elizabeth Bowen once wrote: *"Jealousy is no more than feeling alone against smiling enemies."* Ms. Bowen is saying that in the mind of a jealous person, they sit alone while being surrounded by happy people who are secretly mocking them.

Everyone, at one time or another have been jealous of something or someone. It's a normal human emotion. In some cases, you can't control how you feel. However, you can control how you react. *Jealous Joans* are constantly envious of others for a variety of reasons.

What do you do with a *Jealous Joan*?

o   There is no clear-cut way to address a jealous person. Mainly because there are so many reasons why Joan might be jealous. For example, if Joan is jealous of your lifestyle, there is no way that you will change it to make her more comfortable. Maybe your house is bigger than hers or your car is newer. The best way to approach Joan for either of these is to make sure you don't boast about the house or car when you are in her presence. You should never feel uncomfortable when speaking of your possessions. However, it's "how" you address them that may spur jealousy.

o   If Joan is envious of the relationship between you and your spouse or mate, it's usually because her relationship may not be as solid. Or it may be because she doesn't have a relationship. Remember people who truly care for you and love you are not jealous of you. Sometimes it's better to remove those persons from your life if the jealousy becomes too overbearing.

A Biblical Reference to Consider:

For where jealousy and selfish ambition exist, there will be disorder and every vile practice
James 3:16

Chloe The Competitor

Have you ever been in a competition where you didn't know you were competing? There's a couple who are very close friends of ours. The problem is, everything is a competition to them. Unlike *Jealous Joan* who wants to keep up with the Joneses, *Chloe the Competitor* and her partner Clyde want to compare everything that everyone else has to their own personal belongings. During an overnight stay at our home, Clyde commented on the pancakes that I made for breakfast the next morning. He wanted to know if I used Bisquick for the batter because they were *almost* as fluffy as his. I let him know that I purchase whichever brand happens to be on sale on my trip to the market.

Later that afternoon I had prepared spaghetti for dinner. Chloe made sure to tell me that she uses a different tomato sauce. Therefore, hers has a heartier flavor. I have found that regardless of the topic, they have something better and want to turn everything into a competition. I have no problem with it because I am not competing. But others who have been present quickly become annoyed. Even people that they don't know fall prey to the constant comparisons.

Chloe makes it known that she bakes everything from scratch. GREAT. I am happy for her. But given my hectic schedule, Betty Crocker and Duncan Hines work just fine.

What do you do with a *Chloe*?

o   If *Chloe* is one of your employees, make use of her competitive nature to your advantage. Give her a project that requires her to compete with the company's competitors not her co-workers.

o   However, if there is a job promotion or new position involved, let *Chloe* do her thing if she is not endangering other employees. The competition may put a little fire under a *"Do Nothing Dave"*.

o   If Chloe is a friend, let her know that you are not competing with her. Ask her directly: "Why is everything always a competition with you?" See if that diffuses her competing flames.

A Biblical Reference to Consider:

Do nothing from rivalry or conceit, but in humility count others more significant than yourselves.

Philippians 2:3

Detective Dan

Know someone who investigates everyone's personal information just to be nosy? One day I was having a general discussion with a co-worker. During the conversation I mentioned that Ed, another co-worker had just moved into a new home. Dan immediately sprang into action. He was able to tell me which neighborhood Ed had moved to, his address, and how much the house cost. When he noticed my curious eyes, he responded, "you can find anything on the Internet these days". I was taken so off guard that I was speechless. I then began to wonder if Dan had done his detective work on me. Not that I have anything to hide. But that's not the point.

Detective Dan is always finding juicy bits of information on everyone. But why?

Could it be that Dan's life is just that empty and boring that everyone else's life seems more interesting? Is Dan just nosy and wants to obtain as much information as possible about everyone else?

I never understood such behavior. But here are a few pointers for dealing with a "Detective Dan":

o   Only share information with Dan that you don't mind anyone else knowing.

o   When Dan tries to share confidential information about someone, ask him why he feels the need to share that information. Also, ask him how he knows. If he indicates that he looked it up on Google, ask why. Ask why he feels the need to share.

o   Avoid Dan when he wants to discuss topics that are not comfortable for you. Especially if the information is private and about someone that you both know.

o   If Dan is one of your employees, make sure you impress upon him that disclosing personal information about others is not a part of his job description. The only sensitive information that you should be obtaining or retaining from Dan are those things that pose a threat to the security of the organization/corporation, the privacy of an employee or the confidentiality of a customer.

o   If Dan is a friend, ask him why he is so intent on prying into everyone's business. Let him know that you don't appreciate it and prefer that he doesn't meddle into your business.

A Biblical Reference to Consider:

> *You shall not go around as a slanderer among your people, and you shall not stand up against the life of your neighbor: I am the LORD.*
>
> Leviticus 19:16

Lying Lindsey

Ever met a pathological liar? I am referring to a person who lies for the sake of lying. Eventually you don't believe anything they say.

I have a friend who is married to a *Lindsey*. Lindsey has told so many lies that I don't think he knows the difference between what he has fabricated and the truth. There have been occasions when friends have gathered, and we'd reminisce about "the good old days". Lindsey immediately responds, "I remember that". We know that he couldn't possibly remember the event because it took place before we met him.

A relative had passed away. *Lindsey* and I went to the market to purchase food items to take to the family's home. We decided to stop by the Dollar Tree on the way to the repast to buy an inexpensive cake holder for the chocolate cake that we purchased. Because we had inserted the cake into the holder prior to arriving, a relative asked if Lindsey had baked the cake. Lindsey immediately replied, "Yes".

Both Lindsey and the relative caught my look of disbelief and the relative just walked away shaking her head in disgust. She realized that Lindsey was once again spurring falsehoods. Was there a reason to lie about baking the cake?

My mom used to say that if you'll lie, you'll steal. And if you'll steal, you'll kill. That was her way of letting me and my siblings know that one dishonest act is just as bad as another.

How do you handle *"Lying Lindsey"*?

o Don't handle him. If Lindsey is a friend, be cautious in what you share with him. He will put his twist on anything that he feels is gossip worthy. If Lindsey continually lies, ask yourself why you need him in your life. You can be acquaintances. However, friends are persons with whom you can communicate and share life's experiences. Why waste your time with a person who is constantly lying... for no reason? Not that there is ever a real reason to lie. But why bother?

o If Lindsey is one of your employees, discuss his propensity to lie. Document the discussion and follow up in his performance evaluation.

A dishonest person is a dishonest person. It's just that simple. Remember what my mother said" "If you'll lie, you'll steal. If you'll steal, you'll kill.

A Biblical Reference to Consider:

A false witness will not go unpunished, and he who breathes out lies will perish...
Proverbs 19:9

Sabotaging Shayla

"Sabotaging Shayla" is that friend or co-worker who delights in destroying your reputation. Usually done out of spite or jealousy, Shayla sneaks around until she finds a weakness or mistake that you have made. She then pounces and makes sure to inflate the situation. Because Shayla is a coward, her schemes are carried out behind the scenes, without your knowledge.

She will usually disguise herself as a friend or ally. She extracts just enough information from you to build her case. You may wear better clothes, have a better working relationship with others, have a better appearance or maybe have never done anything to initiate the resentment. She may not like you... just because.

For whatever the reason, Shayla will spend time conjuring up ways to discredit you in the eyes of your peers, friends, co-workers or even your employer. Once she has spurred her bad seeds, she sits back and watches your reputation suffer.

The problem with the *"Sabotaging Shaylas"* of the world is that by the time you find out what has happened, your reputation may already be ruined beyond immediate repair.

When confronted with a *"Sabotaging Shayla":*

o   Try not to be too defensive when defending yourself. This may be hard in some situations. But the cooler you remain, the easier it is to dispel her innuendos.

o   Unless you have a long-standing relationship with your boss, never assume that he or she knows you well enough to dispel accusations from Shayla. If your boss is mature, he or she can usually tell who is being truthful (usually by your history or work ethic). Keep good documentation on all your work.

o   Once you have identified Shayla, send emails following all conversations that are related to projects or tasks shared with her. This is a good practice for any co-worker. It ensures that all parties are informed. Make sure the documentation is clear and concise.

A Biblical Reference to Consider:

> *Lying lips are an abomination to the LORD, but those who act faithfully are his delight.*
> Proverbs 12:22

Candice the Cheerleader

Candice the Cheerleader is that peppy, happy person who is always there to cheer on everyone. "Way to go team!" "Woo Hoo, you're the best!" "I am so happy that you got the promotion."

"Thank you for helping me with my project. You rock!" "I am here for you, girlfriend". "I thank God that you are in my life."

Candice is genuine. She's a cheerful person and a joy to be around. She is usually in a good space and can lift your spirits when you are feeling down in the dumps.

Every office needs a Candice. Every girlfriend circle must have a Candice. Whenever things are falling apart, you can always go to Candice for a quick "pick me up" or a word of encouragement.

The world would be a much better place if there were more people like Candice.

What do you do with the Candice in your life?

o Cherish her. She'll be there for you.

o Be there for her. Candice has days when she will need cheering as well. Everyone has bad days or times when things are not going as planned. Be a cheerleader for Candice when those days occur in her life.

o If you are her manager, make sure you reflect your appreciation for Candice's positive attitude and team like spirit.

o Do not over task her because of her demeanor.

o Do not take advantage of her kindness. Persons with an extremely upbeat personality often become overwhelmed when under extreme pressure.

o Enjoy her energy and keep her in your life. She's usually the type of person who is a lifelong friend.

A Biblical Reference to Consider:

A joyful heart is good medicine.

Psalm 17:22

Backstabbing Bessie

In the late 1970's, R & B group, the OJay's made it plain in their hit single "The Backstabbers". The OJay's said: "They smile in your face, but all the time they want to take your place, the backstabbers".

No truer words have ever been spoken. People who stab you in the back are usually jealous of you and wish they could be in your shoes. They usually pretend to be your friend while secretly wishing they were you.

Backstabbers are sneaky. They watch you. They befriend you. They even imitate you. Bessie may go so far as to dress like you and change her hairstyle to reflect yours. She'll wear similar clothes. Bessie will shop in the same stores as you.

The problem is that because she has become a "so called" friend, you will most likely not notice the behavior at first. You may even take it as a compliment.

Others will see it. They may even try to discretely warn you. However, because of Bessie's uncanny way of befriending you, you may not believe that she's being deceitful. After all, she's your friend.

This one is not so cut and dry. Why? Because, usually by the time you realize that *Bessie* is a *Backstabber*, you've been hurt and may have already ended the relationship. However, if you have not been hurt by her, here are a few pointers for dealing with *Backstabbing Bessie*:

o Let Bessie know that you are aware of her betrayal.

o You can let her know that you are disappointed because you thought she was a dear friend.

o Let her know that she has lost a true friend in you.

o Walk away. Even if she wants to make amends and try again, you can always forgive. However, the trust has been broken.

o If you decide to reignite the friendship. Proceed with extreme caution. People may change. But rarely do they change their true personality. Be extremely careful.

A Biblical Reference to Consider:

A dishonest man spreads strife, and a whisperer separates close friends.

Proverbs 16:28

Indecisive India

Some of my most challenging experiences in both my professional and personal life has been working with people who cannot make a decision. They may be the nicest people on the planet. But when it comes to deciding what to do, they panic. They ask you to make the decision. The *Indecisive India's* of the world can make your life difficult because they often put you in a position to make decisions that you are neither equipped to make nor should be making.

When confronted with an *Indecisive India*:

○ If the issue is personal in nature and involves India, her family or friends, you must take the decision off your shoulder and put it back into her lap. You cannot and should not make life changing decisions for someone else. That's a true recipe for disaster. If for some reason the decision was not the right one or the best decision for the occasion, you will be in the middle of a situation and could be blamed for the outcome.

○ If the issue is work related and you are not the final decision maker, again, place the decision back in India's court. If you are colleagues and need a final resolution, speak with your manager. Never take on full responsibility for someone else's project or task. Again, you will find yourself in the middle of a situation and you may end up bearing the full brunt of the results.

○ Be careful when offering your opinion as well. If at work and you find yourself in a situation where an opinion is required. Make sure you have a clear discussion with India and follow up all points with a detailed email outlining everything that was discussed. NEVER leave any item or part of the discussion open or your suggestion or statements unclear. Make sure to copy everyone involved.

A Biblical Reference to Consider:

> *Be sober-minded; be watchful. Your adversary the devil prowls around like a roaring lion, seeking someone to devour.*

1 Peter 5:8

Annie The Athlete

Annie the Athlete is that one person in the office who is always weight conscience, health conscience and eats all the right foods...always. She wakes up each morning at 5:00 AM and makes her way to the gym where she works out before heading to work. She drinks a puke-colored smoothie for breakfast, puts on her sweats at noon and walks at least a half hour during lunch. She takes the stairs instead of the elevator.

Annie is always full of energy. She never gets sick. She always dresses neatly. Her clothes are always perfectly form fitting. She's usually a joy to be around, except for the fact that she is always trying to get you to join the gym or accompany her to a work out boot camp.

What do you do with *"Annie the Athlete"*?

o   Absolutely nothing. Follow her lead. Most people, including myself, are stuck in the same old rut each day. We make promises to ourselves and others at the beginning of every year to be more active and exercise more. It never works out.

o   Ask Annie for pointers on starting a routine that is easy to "stick to" ... and stick to it.

o   Keep Annie in mind when you feel the urge to skip the gym and head to your local ice cream parlor. Remember her energy level and how nice she looks in her clothes.

o   Compliment Annie on her appearance and her discipline.

o   Visit your physician and obtain your three "B's":

   ~Blood Pressure
   ~Blood Sugar
   ~Body Mass Index

o   Speak with your physician before developing a weight management and health maintenance plan. Then develop a plan that works for you.

o   Let Annie be your incentive and mentor

A Biblical Reference to Consider:

> *Beloved, I pray that all may go well with you and that you may be in good health, as it goes well with your soul.*
>
> 3 John 1:2

Toxic Tommy

Although we see some of *"Toxic Tommy"* in other personality types, there's a distinctive difference. Toxic Tommy tends to force relationships. He knows he's not liked or wanted. However, he tries to influence and push people to allow him into their inner circle. He can be controlling and will lie when necessary to win people over and ensure that others see or understand his point of view.

One of my favorite cartoon characters from childhood was *"Bad Luck Schelprock"*. A rain cloud followed Schelprock wherever he went. People always avoided him because of that cloud. Likewise, drama follows Toxic Tommy. Wherever he goes, you can be assured that drama will follow.

Tommy is never wrong. He talks more that he listens. No one ever explained to him that God purposely proportioned us with one mouth and two ears. Tommy has a habit of spreading negative rumors about others. He loves being the tallest building on the block. However, he usually accomplishes that feat by tearing everyone else down.

How do you deal with Toxic Tommy?

- Stop trying to please Tommy. He realizes that if he pushes the right buttons, because you are a decent person, you will try to make him or anyone else happy. Once you realize that you are dealing with a Toxic Tommy, walk away. You can return if his mood changes to be more positive. If not, keep walking.

- Toxic Tommy will often make you feel defensive. You will feel the need to apologize for something. If an apology is warranted, apologize. However, if you find that you are constantly apologizing because Tommy has made you uncomfortable, don't apologize for something that you didn't do.

- Do not allow Tommy to make you feel small or dampen your spirits in any way. You don't need his or anyone else's approval.

- Always remember that people who really care about you and have your best interest at heart will not go out of their way to hurt or upset you. Remove Tummy from your circle of friends. Move on.

A Biblical Reference to Consider:

Do not be overcome by evil, but overcome evil with good.
                                        Romans 12:21

Listening

One of the most valuable lessons that I have learned is to listen before I speak. The adage that God gave us two ears and one mouth for good reason still holds true. We should use them in proportion and listen more than we speak. If we follow that simple rule this is what will happen:

o   Only you will know when you don't really understand what is being said. That is, unless you prematurely speak up and ruin it for yourself. Remember: It is better to keep silent and be thought a fool, than to speak up and remove all doubt.

o   You will better understand the message that the other person is trying to relay. I have found that when I interrupt another person's conversation, I may have mis-interpreted the point they were trying to make. But if I just take a few additional moments to listen, I can make an informed and more intelligent response.

o   Listening can often defuse the other person's anger. Have you ever noticed that if you keep a cool head when an angry person is speaking that you will learn the reason for their anger? Often you can empathize with them and defuse some of the hostility. However, when you interject on their thought it causes their anger to escalate. Eventually, you both will be in a state of escalation and the conversa-tion will most likely end in hurt feelings or even worse, physical altercation.

o   If you are busy and stop whatever you are doing and genuinely listen to someone, it helps build their confidence and sometimes even their self-esteem. Your ac-tions reflect the fact that you are listening to them and their opinion matters to you. This is very important to everyone from children to adults; from co-workers to employees; and even to spouses or life partners.

o   When you listen, you become more selfless and less selfish. Always remember that what the other person has to say is just as important to them as what you have to say in response. There are times when listening is all a person needs from you. Sometimes no response is needed. They just need to let it out into the at-mosphere. It helps to get whatever is bothering them off their chest.

o   Contain the urge to interrupt the other person's dialog. Let them get it all out.

o   If the conversation is beginning to make you angry, you can stop the person and let them know before you become too irritated. When they stop the conversation, let them know why you interrupted and mention the fact that their words are upsetting to you. Talk it through.

o   Listen. But also notice body language and voice tone. Both are indications of how anxious the person is at that moment.

o   If you begin to fade in and out of the conversation because of boredom or the fact that the person is taking too long to make the point, remind yourself that at this moment, this person's needs and feelings are very important, and you need to stay focused. They need you.

Just LISTEN.

Whether on a job interview, having a conversation with your best friend, speaking with your children or addressing a diverse audience, there are certain things to remember:

- Be Careful When Using Slang. Know your audience. The dictionary is filled with old and very new words. Use them when speaking to an audience. A popular and, or contemporary slang word here and there may bring a favorable response. However, you should "know" the audience well before using slang. When speaking with your kids, be careful not to use too many slang words. We want to instill excellence in the next generation. Using too much slang with kids will often result in them not taking you seriously. The word slang's etymology definition dates back to 1756, where it was referred to as the vocabulary of "low or disreputable" people.   Later slang came to be known as an informal register that members of particular "in-groups" favor in order to establish group identity, exclude outsiders, or both. Slang is used in a way that sometimes people of higher social status will criticize those who use it.

- Be direct in your words. Do not use vague language. "Please finish it as soon as possible!" Finish what? Even though you were in direct communication with someone and you've been working on a project for days, are you certain the person understands your expectations? First, what are they completing? Are they completing the entire project? Are you expecting them to finish the portion that you were just working on together? As soon as possible, for whom? As soon as possible for them may be next week, when you are expecting a finished product by tomorrow morning. Be clear. Be specific. You'll avoid misunderstandings and missed deadlines.

- Avoid "Red Flag" Words. If you are speaking to an adult male, never refer to him as "boy". When speaking to an adult female, never call her a "gal" or "girl". Words can provoke very strong and emotional responses. When speaking to persons of different races, religious affiliations or political beliefs keep your prejudicial jokes and statements to yourself. Consider removing them from your vocabulary and conversations altogether. You never really know who you are talking to and who you may offend.

My brother shared the result of his ancestry/DNA tests and I was shocked at our family's ethnic composition.

o Refrain from using profanity. We all slip up from time to time. However, there is nothing more disgusting than hearing profane language spurring from the mouth of a well-respected female. Men using profanity is disgusting as well. But a beautiful woman in a tailored business suit with a foul mouth is appalling. The listener is immediately turned off and often offended.

o Cut the clichés. If I never hear "well there are six in one hand and half a dozen in the other" ... or "you can't judge a book by its cover" again, it will fine. Clichés are usually over used, old and outdated and you'll appear old and outdated if you continue to use them.

o Keep It Simple & Sweet (KISS). I will never forget that simple expression from Rev. Carl Fogle, one of my father's closest friends. He would joke that when his sermons were too long his wife would write the word KISS on a piece of paper and have an usher slip it to him. As he opened the paper, any onlooker who could view the note would think she was slipping him a sweet love note amid his sermon. When she was actually telling him to *"Keep It Short Stupid"*. He knew what it meant. I softened the message to Keep it Simple and Sweet. Using "BIG" words to make "small" points doesn't make you look intelligent. It usually has the exact opposite effect.

o Stop Using Acronyms and Jargon. Most professions have acronyms and jargon that are used specifically by persons within that occupation. Persons outside of that circle will have no clue about the speaker's intention. Nor do they care in most instances. Also, the same acronyms may have different meanings from one profession to another. For example: In 1955, Joan Woehrmann started her ambulance company in Whittier, California. She used the acronym AIDS (which stood for: Attitude, Integrity, Dependability and Service). Who knew that it would later become a widespread medical outbreak? She eventually changed the name after her drivers were repeatedly taunted because customers thought they catered to persons with the disease. Ms. Woehrmann eventually changed the name of her company to AME.

On a funny note, in 2009 Wisconsin's Tourism Federation changed its abbreviation from WTF. When the Internet turned the term into the expletive abbreviation for "What The F....?", it was time to make a name change. The agency is now known as Tourism Federation of Wisconsin.

Changing the name doesn't always clear up the confusion, however. Iowa's Department of Elder Affairs (DEA), changed its name to the Department on Aging (DOA). That change kept some of the Iowa's elderly up at night. The organization is now known as the IDA (Iowa's Department on Aging).

Just stop the acronyms outside the workplace. They are both annoying and confusing.

o   Refrain from Using Idioms. An idiom is a form of expression natural to a language, person or group of people. One of my most embarrassing moments as a child occurred while on one of our family visits to Baltimore. I had gone to the corner market with a cousin. I was around ten years old. My cousin was about fourteen. I had grown up in a rural area of Virginia. I was already self-conscience about speaking because the Baltimore cousins referred to my brothers and me as being "country". I wanted a Pepsi. So, I asked what type of sodas they had. My cousin immediately embarrassed me by asking why in the world I wanted baking soda. I told her I wanted a Pepsi Cola. She said, "Then ask for a Pepsi or a pop! No one calls "pop", "soda". Each region has its own words and phrases. Refrain from using idioms outside of your very close social circle.

o   Cut Down on the Euphemisms. Euphemisms are polite expressions that are used in place of words that are harsh or unpleasant. One of the most irritating euphemisms that I remember hearing as a child was my grandmother's way of indicating that a family member was pregnant. The relative was "in a family way". The craziest euphemism that I heard as an adult came from a shy young man who was trying to impress me. He asked if he could borrow "my leaded writing utensil". Of course, he wanted to use my pencil. I knew what he meant. But a couple of coworkers who heard him immediately laughed and embarrassed him for his words. As seen in both examples, euphemisms can cause the listener to be confused. Make your point. Be direct. Don't gloss over what you are trying to say. Just say it.

NOTES

References

www.mindtickle.com/blog/10-millennial-personality-traits-he-managers-cant-ignore/

http://waynet.hubgpages.com/hub/9-Ways-to-deal-with-a-nagging-wife

www.thebalancecareers.com/common-characteristices-of-generation-x-professionals

www.forbes.com/sites/jacquelynsmith/2013/09/09/8-tips-or-dealing-with-a-know-it-all-coworker

Smart Moves, Deep, Sam & Sussman, Lyle, Addison-Wesley Publishing Company, Inc. Reading Massachusetts, 1990.

www.forbes.come/sites/lizray/2016/01/01/five-habits-of-controlling -people/

www.scienceofpeople.com/toxic-people/

www.heysigmund.com/toxic-people/

www.purposefairy.com

www.quickanddirty.tips.com

www.epiceveryrep.com

www.skillboosters.com

www.ingramcontent.com/pod-product-compliance
Lightning Source LLC
Chambersburg PA
CBHW081241090426
42738CB00016B/3369